STRUGGLE WELL AT WORK

POSITIVE MENTAL HEALTH STRATEGIES FOR A FLOURISHING WORKFORCE

MICHAEL DICKERSON

Endorsements

"Michael Dickerson has written a must-read for anyone who seeks to better understand the importance of mental health in the workplace. Read this book and you will learn from the best how to enhance your mental wellbeing and that of those you work with."
—Taylor York, YMCA Executive Director

"I have devoted my career to helping create great business cultures, which is all about improving employee engagement. Michael gives great, practical advice on how to address mental wellness in the workplace in *Struggle Well at Work*. If you can help your employees become more mentally healthy, you will improve their life, their resilience, and their engagement. That sounds like the kind of win-win situation business leaders talk about finding all the time, right? If you want a great culture, you cannot ignore the mental health of your employees."
—Frank Smith, President of Mosaic Personnel Solutions

"This is an insightful book on workplace mental health. Michael draws from real-world experience and research to provide actionable steps for leaders and managers. This is a very valuable resource, and I believe this book will make a great contribution to improving employees' overall mental health and wellbeing."
—Tameka Bowen, Licensed Professional Counselor

"One of Michael's many gifts is his ability to empower others to make positive changes regarding their mental well-being. Through chapter checkpoints, reflection questions and key takeaways, the actionable format of *'Struggle Well at Work'* encourages readers to consider how they, as an employee or a manager, can implement immediate positive strategies to improve both their work and personal lives. Michael has long been a wealth of knowledge for working parents in the Oklahoma City metro and beyond, and his new book gives even more individuals the ability to benefit from his wisdom, encouragement, and positivity."
—Erin Page, Managing Editor, Metro Family Magazine

"Mental Health has been a hot topic in recent years and while there are still stigmas surrounding mental illness and well-being, Michael Dickerson aims to break down barriers by providing tangible tools and strategies to help the workforce flourish. A new generation is entering the workforce and with this paradigm shift comes the desire to thrive. *Struggle Well at Work* puts organizations in the driver's seat, with intention, to effect positive and inclusive behavior."
—Amy M. Le, CEO of Quill Hawk Publishing

Struggle Well at Work

Positive Mental Health Strategies for a Flourishing Workforce

International rights and foreign translation are available only through negotiation with Boundbrook Publishing, LLC.

ISBN: 979-8-2182497-4-8

Printed in the United States of America

To my incredible family and steadfast friends, your encouragement has been a driving force behind the creation of this book.

CONTENTS

Introduction

As I embarked on my professional journey after college, I found myself in a role as a social worker working in a program with youth and young adults who faced mental health challenges and teenage parenthood. This opportunity allowed me to make a meaningful impact in my community, and I discovered I had a natural talent for building relationships and teaching mental health and life skills to youth. Supported by a manager who valued work-life balance and nurtured my growth, I thrived in an organization that prioritized employee wellbeing and a positive company culture.

However, as fate would have it, the program lost its funding after five years, and I faced the unsettling prospect of unemployment. Soon enough, I was recruited by another organization that was similar to my previous job but strictly focused on teaching life skills to young individuals. Excitement filled me as I anticipated continuing my passion for educating and supporting youths. Unfortunately, my enthusiasm soon dissipated when I found myself trapped in an unhealthy work environment with a toxic organizational culture. Communication breakdowns with my manager became the norm, which left me feeling disconnected and out of the loop. I was subjected to constant micromanagement and criticized for deviating from the prescribed curriculum, despite receiving positive feedback from the youths I taught. To make matters worse, my team members began undermining my work and gossiping behind my back.

The toll this took on my wellbeing extended far beyond the workplace. Excessive working hours and an inflexible schedule prevented me from attending important family commitments, leading to strained relationships and mounting burnout. The toxicity of my professional life spilled over into my personal life, eroding my mental health and even causing physical symptoms like back spasms, leaving me feeling disconnected from my former self.

Recognizing the profound impact of this stressful work environment, I wanted to reclaim the sense of fulfillment and flourishing I had experienced in my previous role. The need for a healthy work-life balance and a supportive organizational culture became apparent, not only for my well-being but also for my overall happiness and success. Over the next several months, I faced a period of transition, relying on staffing agencies and taking up short-term training contract jobs while searching for a full-time position. Determined to find a healthier and more positive organization, I resolved to be more selective and thorough in my search. As time went on, I noticed a positive change in my mental health, realizing just how much my previous job had negatively impacted my overall mental health.

Eventually, an opportunity presented itself: a full-time position in the mental health field that aligned perfectly with my skills and aspirations for professional growth. Although my mental health was improving, I still carried the trust issues that stemmed from my previous experience, which hindered my ability to fully engage and excel in my new role. However, during a one-on-one meeting with my manager, something extraordinary happened. He genuinely asked me how he could support my success in the job, and at that moment, I opened up about my past work experience and its impact on my mental health. To my surprise and immense gratitude, my manager took my words to heart. He went above and beyond to create a positive environment for both me and our team. Even to this day, he continues to be a supportive mentor, offering guidance not only in my professional life but also in my personal journey. Despite the challenges I faced in that job, I am forever thankful for being part of a team and organization that prioritized my wellbeing.

Why Mental Health in the Workplace Matters

This is why I firmly believe that workplace mental health matters. Throughout my 14+ years in the mental health field training professionals, consulting with organizations, sitting on boards as a mental health advocate, and engaging with youth and young adults, I have witnessed firsthand the stark contrast between positive and toxic work cultures. The organizations that place a premium on their employees' mental health and wellbeing consistently come out on top in the long run. They have committed, loyal, and happy employees who speak highly of their companies to friends and acquaintances outside of the workplace. While no company is perfect and challenges will always exist, fostering a positive environment where employees can thrive and be productive is achievable for every organization that values workplace mental health.

The passion that fuels my advocacy for workplace mental health stems from both my personal experiences and discussions with others who have been impacted by their work environments. Even simple conversations can provide deep insights into the state of one's mental health in the workplace. The most enlightening stories often come from friends, colleagues, and family members who candidly share how their jobs affect their mental wellbeing.

The question then arises: *Why does mental health in the workplace matter so much?*

- It humanizes the workforce
- Every organization bears a moral obligation to care for its employees
- Performance improves when employees are mentally healthy
- Job satisfaction is a fundamental aspiration for employees

First and foremost, it humanizes the workforce. Creating an environment that values people as unique individuals with diverse emotional needs, values, and aspirations is crucial. Treating employees as more than mere cogs in a machine and instead appreciating the contributions they bring to the table promotes empathy, compassion, and support for those who may struggle at various points in their careers.

Secondly, every organization bears a moral obligation to care for the wellbeing of its employees. This encompasses promoting physical, emotional, and mental wellbeing at work. By fostering a positive environment, organizations contribute to employee wellbeing, which in turn builds a thriving workplace where individuals can reach their full potential. This also means actively reducing stress, preventing burnout, and creating positive experiences for employees through supportive management practices.

Thirdly, when individuals are mentally and emotionally well, their performance improves. Companies aspire for their employees to achieve organizational goals, but to attain that, employees' personal and psychological needs must be met, enabling them to perform at their best. Encouraging employees to practice self-care and accommodating individuals with more significant and severe mental health challenges are vital aspects of creating an environment where individuals can thrive and excel in.

Lastly, in today's professional landscape, job satisfaction is a fundamental aspiration for employees. They seek fulfillment, not just in terms of a good salary and benefits, but also in achieving work-life balance, accessing career growth opportunities, and being part of a positive work environment. All these factors contribute to an employee's overall wellbeing at work. When individuals feel a sense of belonging and security, they become more confident and productive, fostering a mutually beneficial relationship between the employee and the organization.

How This Book Will Help You

Imagine an ideal workplace where employees flourish, productivity soars, and your company consistently surpasses its goals. Envision a culture of well-being that permeates every aspect of your organization. What if I told you that this ideal is within your reach? This book serves as a practical guide to help you, your organization, and your employees thrive, cultivating a culture of wellbeing that leads to success.

My objective for writing this book is to assist leaders, managers, and employees in comprehending the significance of workplace mental health and discovering strategies to enhance employee wellbeing. As a mental health practitioner, I believe in bridging the gap between science and practice. I firmly believe that true understanding comes from applying knowledge and ideas in real-world situations. Therefore, I aim to provide you with a roadmap of proven methods that effectively improve employee wellbeing and foster a flourishing workforce. Throughout this book, I will explore the intersectionality of mental health, positive psychology, and workplace culture. I understand the challenges and struggles individuals face in their professional lives, and I firmly believe that one of the most impactful ways to support them is by prioritizing their wellbeing and facilitating their success on the job.

In the following chapters, you will gain a deeper understanding of employee mental health. We will delve into the definition of workplace mental health and wellbeing, while exploring their interconnectedness. I will share insights and ideas on how to promote employee wellbeing, emphasizing the importance of positive mental health. Moreover, we will explore why workplace mental health is crucial for organizational health, productivity, and overall success. By understanding employee wellbeing, leaders, managers, and employees will realize that small changes can significantly improve it, and in turn, create a more positive work experience. Ultimately, we will discover that when individuals have positive experiences and good mental health in the workplace, job satisfaction soars.

This book's strength lies in its practical strategies and checkpoints for both organizational and employee interventions. As you progress, you will discover that fostering a predominantly positive experience at work enhances happiness, while emphasizing social connections and meaningful work aligned with personal values contributes to thriving. Although this book does not solely rely on scientific research, many of the ideas, strategies, and interventions are evidence-based. While the field of workplace mental health is evolving rapidly, rest assured that the strategies presented here are tried, tested, and proven to enhance your workforce. Together, let's embark on this journey toward creating a flourishing workplace, a place where both employees and organizations thrive, achieving sustainable success through prioritizing mental health and wellbeing.

CHAPTER 1

The Middle Child of Mental Health:
Languishing

The Middle Child of Mental Health: Languishing

"Languishing dulls your motivation, disrupts your ability to focus, and triples the odds that you'll cut back on work. It appears to be more common than major depression, and in some ways, it may be a bigger risk factor for mental illness."

—Adam Grant, Organizational Psychologist and Bestselling Author

Recently, I reconnected with my good friend Tony over dinner. At first, he raved about his company and coworkers, but later on, he admitted he felt empty inside and worried he wasn't living up to his full potential at work. He also confided that he feels trapped in his current role and burned out—mentally, physically, *and* emotionally. His professional struggles were beginning to spill over into his personal life, so he knew it was time for a change. As I listened, I quickly realized he was *languishing*. Tony felt he was living a life of quiet despair. He was consumed with these emotions and desperately wanted to overcome them so he could live up to his potential.

What Is Languishing?

Languishing refers to a state of:

- Emptiness

- Restlessness
- Void
- Stagnation
- Lack of purpose

As the pandemic persisted in 2021, professor and organizational psychologist Adam Grant wrote an article in *The New York Times* entitled "There's a Name for the 'Blah' You're Feeling: It's Called Languishing." This article resonated with the majority of those who read it because they finally had the language to describe how they were feeling. The writing was on the wall: A huge percentage of the population was languishing—especially in the workplace.

In my role as a mental health professional, I'm troubled to see so much of the modern workforce in a state of languishing because it's one of the primary drivers of job dissatisfaction. So what's the root of this crisis? It's complex, but in short: Employees want more from their work than just a paycheck. Much like Tony, they want to feel like they're living up to their fullest potential and thriving at work.

Languishing doesn't just affect the employee, either. This state of mind is often counterproductive to their company's goals because employees who are languishing cannot do their best work, plain and simple. Many times, when we think about mental health in the workplace, it's pretty black and white. There are the employees who are mentally ill and the ones who are flourishing. However, the reality is: that languishing poses the biggest threat to a company's productivity.

The Overlooked Middle Child

If the workplace mental health continuum were a family, "languishing" would be the middle child between "flourishing" and "depression." In families, the middle child is often unintentionally ignored. And in workplaces, languishing employees often do not get the attention they deserve. That's because their leadership teams are focused on addressing issues with employees who are struggling with severe mental illnesses— or awarding high praise to those employees who are thriving in their role. However these two groups do not represent the majority. So how can leaders and managers help those employees who languishing? What can we do help employees flourish? We'll answer these questions in later chapters!

Where Languishing Fits in the Mental Health Continuum

The Professor Corey Keyes of Emory University in Georgia introduced the concept of languishing in the Journal of Health and

Social Research 2002 article; he describes the "presence of complete mental health" as "flourishing," and the "absence of complete mental health" as "languishing." According to 2021 research from Better Help, 55% percent of employees are languishing—and I'd imagine that the rate is far higher today. In Keyes' mental health continuum graph, you can explore the relationship between mental illness, mental health, flourishing, and languishing. It's important to note that employees who are languishing do not have high rates of mental illness, but they also lack complete mental health.

Another way to think of employees who are languishing is that they're in "neutral," much like a car. The only way to get the car going is to start moving forward. Once the car is moving forward, it'll eventually drive at the right speed. If we were to use a scale from -10 (severe mental illness) to +10 (flourishing), languishing employees would be at 0. The hope for employers is to move these employees from 0 to +7. That way, the employees become more productive at work and are not at risk for depression. Because in times of stress, languishing can quickly morph into full-blown depression.

When Languishing Becomes Depression

According to the Center for Workplace Mental Health, workplace depression costs American employers on average $44 billion each year in lost productivity. When languishing workers do not get the help they need, it only gets worse—and mental illnesses like depression can take a devastating toll on employee motivation and healthcare costs for a company. This is why languishing employees pose a major threat to an organization's bottom line. To combat this, mental health education programs and comprehensive healthcare plans are imperative.

Here are some additional facts about depression in the workplace from Mental Health America:

- Depression ranks among the top three workplace problems following family crisis and stress.
- Almost 15% of those suffering from severe depression will die by suicide.
- 3% of total short-term disability days are due to depressive disorders.

Absenteeism & Presenteeism

When enough individual employees are languishing or depressed, their organization experiencing high levels of absenteeism and presenteeism. Presenteeism occurs when employees are technically "at work" but not fully present and living up to their potential. Ever had a coworker who showed up only to do the bare minimum? On the other hand, absenteeism occurs when employees frequently miss work because of illness, mental health issues, or burnout. When a colleague on your team calls into work three or four times every month, it impacts the whole team's ability to get work done. Therefore, it affects the productivity of the organization as a whole.

According to a report by Gallup, employers are losing $450–500 billion a year in productivity. I believe the lion's share of this loss stems from presenteeism and absenteeism in the workplace due to languishing. Most employees want to enjoy their job. They don't want to feel burned out, and they especially don't want to hurt their team or organization. Their employers can help them by understanding the significance of positive mental health—and strategies for achieving it—which we'll cover in a later chapter.

Summary

Employees who are languishing will not reach their full potential at work. At best, they'll do bare the minimum until they eventually become burned out or trigger a serious mental illness like depression. In this new age of work, employers must not overlook these serious issues. Understanding the framework of mental health at work and how we got here in the first place will be a vital part of developing the interventions and strategies that work best. This means we need to explore the foundational principles of flourishing!

Chapter Takeaways

- Languishing is the state of emptiness, restlessness, and lack of purpose that many employees experience, impacting their job satisfaction and overall wellbeing.

- The majority of the modern workforce is languishing, leading to decreased productivity and dissatisfaction in the workplace.

- Languishing employees often receive less attention compared to high performers or those with a severe mental illness, creating a gap in support.

- Languishing can escalate into depression if left unaddressed, resulting in significant costs for employers and negative impacts on employee motivation.

- Understanding and promoting positive mental health is crucial for addressing languishing and creating interventions to support employees.

Checkpoint

1. Can you think of a time when you languished as an employee? Are you there now? What kind of support did you get? What kind did you need?

2. What percentage of employees in your organization are languishing, in your opinion? Why do you think this is? How can you help?

CHAPTER 2

Mental Health in the Workplace

Mental Health in the Workplace

"Mental health needs a great deal of attention. It's the final taboo, and it needs to be faced."
—Adam Ant, Musician and Actor

Chris is a 28-year-old employee who worked at a manufacturing company in a suburban area just outside of Houston. He liked his job due to the good pay, proximity to the small town in Texas where he grew up, and the friendships he formed with his coworkers throughout his five years there. He lives with his girlfriend, Ashley, who is currently seven months pregnant. Over the last couple months, Chris' department experienced high turnover, leaving him to juggle the increased workload and longer hours. As his stress level multiplies at work, his stress at home followed — and the thought of having a new baby weighed heavily on his mind.

To decompress after work, Chris enjoyed having drinks with his coworkers. He was known for his fun-loving spirit and love for entertaining his friends, however, his drinking escalated, spiraling out of control. His drinking sessions extended far beyond the usual happy hours and late into night, despite knowing he had to be at work early the next morning. In addition, his girlfriend

Ashley felt incredibly neglected and unsupported during the late stages of her pregnancy due to his drinking.

Before long, every one of his colleagues was aware of his alcohol abuse. When Chris is *at* work, he's very good at his job. The problem was, his drinking made him either chronically late or absent from work due to oversleeping or crippling hangovers. Yet even though everyone knows about his drinking problem, none of his colleagues had ever approached him about it. Other than the occasional slap on the wrist for his tardiness or absences, his supervisor constantly gave him a pass because he was such a great worker otherwise (and, frankly, the team remained understaffed). Although his coworkers and supervisor worried about him, they believed it wasn't their place to confront him about his destructive relationship with alcohol.

Much like it was within many other workplaces, talking about mental health matters wasn't a part of Chris manufacturing company's culture—except for the occasional water cooler gossip, which was more harmful than good. Instead, they swept issues like these under the rug. This dynamic, unfortunately remains a common one.

Chapter 2: Mental Health in the
Workplace

Cultural Taboos in the Workplace and Beyond

This phenomenon isn't unique to just workplaces either. Throughout the last half-century, most people didn't speak about mental health much, if at all. If they did, they probably disclosed a personal struggle with mental illness like depression and anxiety, which are the most common two. Culturally, the typical "prescription" for dealing with a mental disorder in the past was to keep it a secret—hidden from everyone but your family. Up until the early nineties, most people did not sufficiently understand mental health unless they worked in a related field. Then, new technology like the internet emerged. Suddenly, you could do research on mental health. While that came with risks for some people (such as self-diagnosis and paranoia), but overall, this democratization of information was a largely positive development.

Like any major cultural shift, it was slow going—and our workplaces are still lagging in the mental health sphere. Because many employees don't even know where to begin with their mental health, they often take the path of least resistance like Chris' workplace did: overlooking or ignoring mental health issues in the hopes they'll go away on their own. But they rarely do. Even if it isn't explicitly stated, it's implied: Keep your struggles to yourself and *out* of the workplace—much like politics and religion. However, this approach ends up being counterproductive to what they are trying to accomplish in their organization.

Why Mental Health Conversations Belong in the Workplace

Mental health discussions belong in the workplace because mental health issues are already there, which is evident in Chris' situation. According to a 2022 report by the American Psychological Association, the majority of employees deeply value mental health support in the workplace. The report, which examined over 2,000 working adults, found that 81% of U.S. workers are looking for jobs with companies that care about their mental health. According to the results, many of the participants traced their mental health problems back to the workplace, especially toxic environments.

Like almost everything else, mental health issues don't happen in a vacuum, and the research is clear: When employees are mentally healthy, they're 13% more productive and 38% more engaged than those who are mentally unwell, so they perform better. Most organizations want to succeed, but to do so, they must get the best out of their employees. This can only happen when an employee can be their best self at work. But what does "mentally healthy" even mean—or look like?

Mental Illness vs. Mental Health

Often when news media reports on a story about someone who's experiencing depression, anxiety, or bipolar disorder, they use the word "mental health" when they mean "mental illness." These two terms are *not* interchangeable, but they *are* two sides of the same coin. In reality, mental health is a spectrum—like most things are.

When we focus on mental disorders like depression or anxiety, we're operating under what many mental health experts call the *disease model*. Not only is this approach short-sighted, but it's the one that still reigns supreme within many organizations. In the workplace, mental health is most strongly associated with employee stress and burnout—the *problems*, not the *solutions*. What's typically left out of the conversation is the *positive* side of mental health.

Redefining Mental Health

The World Health Organization defines mental health as "a state of wellbeing in which every individual realizes his or her potential, can cope with daily stresses in life, can work productively and fruitfully, and can make a contribution to his or her community." Not only does this description demonstrate what flourishing looks like, which we'll cover in a later chapter, but it's also a great checklist for employers.

Summary

Mental Health issues are often ignored, with the hope that they will resolve themselves, a mindset counterproductive to a healthy work environment. Conversations around mental health are essential in the workplace. Most employees value mental health support in their jobs, with many tracing their mental health concerns back to a toxic work environment. By redefining mental health as a state of optimal well-being and productivity, organizations are better equipped to ensure their employees flourish and contribute effectively.

Chapter Takeaways

- Workplace cultures often avoid discussions about mental health, leading to a lack of support and understanding.

- Employees value mental health support in the workplace, and their mental health problems are often linked to their toxic work environments.

- Prioritizing mental health increases productivity, engagement, and overall performance.

- Mental health should be understood as a spectrum, encompassing both mental illness and positive wellbeing.

- Creating environments that promote mental health can enable individuals to realize their potential, cope with stress, and contribute to their communities.

Checkpoint

1. On a scale of 1-5, with 1 being "poor" and 5 being "optimal," rate your own and/or your average employee's ability to:

   A. Realize their potential: _____

   B. Cope with stressors in daily life: _____

   C. Work productively and fruitfully: _____

   D. Make a contribution to their community: _____

2. What's the dynamic like in your workplace? Do your coworkers open up about their mental health? Do you feel safe discussing yours? Why/why not?

3. When you hear the term "mental health," what comes to mind?

4. Would you consider yourself to be mentally healthy? Why/why not? And what needs to happen to bring you a healthier well-being?

CHAPTER 3

Reducing Mental Health Stigma in the Workplace

Reducing Mental Health Stigma in the Workplace

"Mental illness is nothing to be ashamed of, but stigma and bias shame us all."

—Bill Clinton, Former President of the United States

The biggest barrier to workplace wellbeing is the stigmas (negative attitudes and beliefs) that are associated with mental health. This means that if an employee is struggling with mental illness, like Chris, who is in recovery for substance abuse, they might experience stereotypes and discriminatory practices in the workplace. Chris might be labeled an "alcoholic," which could make it difficult for him to perform well in his job, especially if his colleagues lack sufficient understanding of recovery and addiction. When an employee is labeled or stereotyped, not only is it hurtful, but it reduces them to just one aspect of their identity as well. Instead, we should view every employee as a whole person, recognizing that they are much more than their mental health condition. So, how can leaders and managers combat mental health stigma in the workplace?

Educate Employees About Mental Health

Providing mental health education to all staff is an essential first step to decreasing stigma. By implementing comprehensive education and training programs, you can raise awareness about mental health issues, fostering a more informed and empathetic workforce. This can cover a wide array of topics, such as understanding mental health symptoms and signs, providing mental health training for managers, learning how to communicate effectively with colleagues struggling with mental health issues, and fostering empathy for coworkers dealing with mental illness. Employees have the knowledge and understanding about mental health to empower them to support their colleagues and promote a more supportive work environment.

Every organization needs to tailor education and training programs to their specific needs, whether that be workshops, seminars, online resources, or another type. It's also important for employees to be able to engage in genuine discussions, ask questions, share experiences, and understand the misconceptions surrounding mental health. By investing in mental health education, you demonstrate a commitment to the wellbeing of your employees and create a foundation for a workplace culture that prioritizes mental health support and understanding. However, mental health education and training alone are not sufficient for tangible change to occur in most workplaces, so involving a mental health coach is the most effective approach. This can significantly enhance the wellbeing of employees and help them apply the knowledge they've gained from mental health education and training.

Change the Conversation Around Mental Health

Shifting the language your staff uses about mental health is crucial for creating a more supportive and inclusive environment. By transitioning from stigmatizing to compassionate terms, organizations can promote mental wellbeing and foster a healthier workplace culture. For example, rather than referring to someone as "crazy" or "unstable," use phrases like "experiencing a mental health challenge" or "seeking support for their wellbeing." Nobody uses perfect language about mental health at all times, but the more familiar employees become with the terminology, the more naturally it will be incorporated into daily conversations. This normalization can help break down barriers and alleviate fears and shame associated with mental health struggles. Using inclusive language that acknowledges the prevalence of mental health challenges and underscores the importance of seeking support can create a safe space for employees to share their experiences and access the resources they need. By modifying the workplace language around mental health, organizations can contribute to a culture that values employees' mental wellbeing, supports their journey towards recovery, and promotes a more compassionate workplace.

Enhance Leadership Buy-in About Mental Health

The truth is, if your organization's leadership team doesn't buy in, destigmatizing mental health in the workplace simply won't occur. When leaders actively support and advocate for mental health initiatives, it sends a compelling message to employees: Their mental wellbeing is valued and prioritized. This level of engagement helps break down the stigma surrounding mental health and encourages employees to feel safe and supported when seeking help or openly discussing their mental health challenges.

Moreover, leadership buy-in sets the tone for the entire organization. I'm familiar with two organizations where their leadership has actively championed workplace mental health. In the first organization, they held a panel discussion featuring members of the executive leadership team who either shared personal mental health challenges or had received consent to discuss a family member's struggles. Employees were able to ask questions and engage in open dialogue with the leadership. In the second organization, a director initiated a monthly lunch-and-learn session featuring mental health and wellbeing speakers who engaged with their teams. I recently spoke to a group of bankers during a monthly mental health initiative, my presentation centered on methods to enhance their self-care practices and strategies to elevate their overall well-being. These initiatives, led by leadership, showcased the importance of their influence. Employees are more likely to engage in their work and collaborate effectively when they feel understood and supported by their leaders in relation to their mental health needs.

Leadership buy-in also plays a vital role in implementing mental health policies and programs within the organization. When leaders recognize the importance of mental health and provide the necessary resources and support, it enables the development and implementation of initiatives such as workplace mental health and wellbeing programs.

Launch Organizational Campaigns About Workplace Mental Health

The City of Saint Paul employs over 3,000 individuals, with 98% of its workforce unionized, and the city takes pride in fostering a strong community and addressing challenges head-on. Representatives from several departments grew concerned about the wellbeing of city employees, particularly after noticing an alarming trend of annual suicides spanning various departments—from the fire department to public libraries. Aware that many employees were grappling with depression and other serious mental health issues, the city decided to launch a workplace mental health initiative. They trained supervisors, bolstered their

Employee Assistance Program (EAP), sent HR professionals to mental health first-aid training, and hosted a community dialogue at a museum where attendees could openly discuss and interact with an exhibit on mental health. Organizational campaigns like this one can be potent tools for raising awareness and cultivating supportive cultures. These campaigns strive to dismantle the stigma surrounding mental health and create an environment where employees feel comfortable seeking help and support. By involving employees from all levels in these initiatives, organizations can demonstrate their commitment to prioritizing mental wellbeing and foster a greater sense of unity and shared responsibility.

Additionally, such campaigns can leverage communication channels like internal newsletters, intranet platforms, or social media to share relevant resources, tips, and personal stories about mental health. Through these channels, organizations can reach a wider audience and ensure the message of mental health support and awareness is consistently reinforced. Encouraging employees to share their own stories can further contribute to reducing stigma, as it shows that mental health challenges are common and seeking help is a sign of strength.

Summary

Organizational campaigns about mental health are essential for creating a workplace culture that values and supports employees' mental wellbeing. By actively engaging employees, providing education and resources, and encouraging open dialogue, organizations can foster a positive and inclusive environment where mental health is recognized and prioritized. There's no one-size-fits-all solution for reducing mental health stigma in the workplace, but these strategies are a good place to start. It's crucial to remember that anyone experiencing mental health challenges at work is a person deserving of respect. People are complex, and there are many facets to each individual. The workplace should be an environment where people are treated holistically and not labeled or condemned for their illnesses.

Chapter Takeaways

- Negative attitudes and beliefs are the primary obstacle to achieving workplace wellbeing, overcoming stereotypes, and ending discriminatory practices.

- Initiate comprehensive mental health education and training to raise awareness and create an informed and supportive workforce.

- Leadership engagement is crucial. Active support and advocacy for mental health initiatives encourage stigma-free atmospheres and fosters the safety needed for open discussions.

- Implement workplace-wide campaigns like the City of Saint Paul's initiative to raise awareness and destigmatize mental health.

Checkpoint

1. In what way(s) does your organization currently address employee mental health issues? How could you improve this approach?

2. Reflecting on the language section, what changes could your organization make to promote more positive, supportive discussions about mental health?

3. What communication channels could your organization harness for sharing mental health resources, tips, and/or personal stories?

CHAPTER 4

What is "Optimal?"

What Is "Optimal?"

"The aim of positive psychology is to catalyze a change in psychology from a preoccupation with repairing only the worst things in life to also building the best qualities in life."
–Martin Seligman, Director of Penn Positive Psychology Center and American Psychologist

In the late 19th century, no one was praised for their insights into human motivation and employee productivity more than Frederick Taylor. "Taylorism," also known as scientific management, focuses on analyzing and streamlining employee workflows. Taylor's strategies, including breaking tasks down into efficient and repeatable steps, were instrumental in enhancing industrial production, notably at the Ford Motor Company, where he advocated for training and evaluating employees on what he considered to be scientific methods for achieving optimal performance. For example, he timed rail workers loading iron onto cars and adjusted processes if their productivity lapsed.

However, modern critiques of Taylorism argue that its mechanistic approach is too short-sighted, dehumanizing employees by treating them as mere cogs in the machine. Although Taylorism improved organizational efficiency, it failed to consider employees' need for fulfillment and wellbeing. At the time Taylorism gained traction, psychology was in its earliest stages, and maximizing profits was often the primary corporate focus. Fortunately, we recognize the significant role psychology plays in employee motivation and wellbeing in the 21st century.

The Birth of Traditional Psychology

The roots of psychology can be traced back to Ancient Greece, where early thinkers became fascinated by the inner workings of the mind and its impact on behavior. The Greeks laid the groundwork for understanding the mind-body connection, and the philosopher, Plato, theorized on the soul being the source of the mind, body and human behavior, which paved the way for much of modern psychology.

Progress in the 20th Century

Throughout the 20th century, the field of psychology primarily revolved around three subjects:

- Human behavior
- Mental health
- Personal development and motivation

Several key figures and approaches emerged, including Sigmund Freud's psychoanalysis, Ivan Pavlov and B.F. Skinner's behaviorism, and Carl Jung's analytical psychology. Over time, however, psychology leaned heavily toward diagnosing and treating mental health issues, sidelining the personal development piece. Humanistic psychology, which emphasized the importance of personal growth and self-actualization, eventually challenged this trend toward the "disease model" we discussed in earlier chapters. Pioneered by the likes of Abraham Maslow and Carl Rogers, humanistic psychology delved into aspects like motivation, self-esteem, and the search for meaning. Despite these contributions, humanistic psychology eventually faded, and traditional psychology regained its stronghold. That is, until the rise of positive psychology in the early 1990s through the work of Martin Seligman.

Martin Seligman, often referred to as the "father of positive psychology" gained prominence for his significant contributions in the field. He is widely recognized for his research on the concept of learned helplessness, which occurs when an individual perceives a lack of control over their circumstances, leading them to adopt behaviors, thoughts, and emotions that reinforce their sense of powerlessness. In response to this, Seligman shifted his focus towards its opposite-optimism. He developed a framework for learned optimism and simultaneously laid the foundation for positive psychology, a field dedicated to exploring optimal human functioning.

Positive Psychology in the Workplace

Positive psychology strives to understand optimal human functioning by exploring the positive aspects of people and the elements that enable them to flourish or thrive. This discipline, which is humanistic psychology's little brother, places greater emphasis on sound evidence. In fact, it got its start from collecting research. Over time, it's evolved to focus on finding meaningful ways to drive positive, practical changes that improve the lives of individuals, institutions, and workplaces.

Throughout this book, we'll delve into the research and practices of positive psychology—along with how to apply them within the modern workplace. Although our work environments are rapidly changing and heavily influenced by technological advancements, positive psychology continually presents new and relevant research insights on leadership, management, coaching, and organizational development. Its power lies in its capacity to provide a scientific framework for optimizing work performance and helping organizations cultivate positive cultures.

Don't mistake positive psychology for "toxic" positivity. Unlike toxic positivity, positive psychology doesn't ignore the negative experiences that happen in the workplace, nor does it promise that every employee will flourish. Instead, it offers evidence-based strategies for enhancing the workplace experience. By providing the right environment and interventions, workplaces can become spaces where positive interactions are the norm. Every employee should have the chance to become their best self at work. And when individuals are at their best, there's often a positive ripple effect that's felt throughout the entire organization.

Leveraging Your Strengths

Anytime I ask people about their strengths, I get a kick out of the responses I receive. Most individuals look as startled as a deer in the headlights as they scramble to come up with an answer. Others place their hands on their hips or roll their eyes and respond with a sarcastic "I don't know." That's because our culture almost prioritizes modesty to a fault, often to the point where recognizing our strengths becomes a great challenge. However, understanding your strengths at work is a crucial component of professional development, revealing what energizes us, which job roles are right for us, and which ways of completing tasks are most efficient for us. Sadly, research shows that only 17% of individuals are harnessing their strengths at work daily, which is a shame because when we tap into our unique strengths, we feel more motivated, perform better, and are more likely to achieve our goals.

How, then, can you help your employees uncover their own strengths? Start with an assessment! The VIA (or Value in Action)

Character Strengths is a free foundational strength assessment and positive psychology favorite. It scores individuals on 24 universal character strengths, including the love of learning, curiosity, forgiveness, justice, creativity, honesty, gratitude, and more. This assessment can help you pinpoint your core values and what energizes you—both in life and at work. Other strength assessments, like the Strengths Finder or Strengths Profile, provide a more workplace-specific understanding of your talents and abilities and shed light on your top core competencies. Regardless of which tool your team uses, the research is clear: When employees discover and leverage their strengths, they perform their best at work—and organizational outcomes improve as a result!

How to Promote Wellbeing in Your Workplace

A discussion around employee mental health and optimal workplace performance naturally leads to the concept of wellbeing, which encompasses:

- Physical health
- Emotional satisfaction
- Financial stability
- Mental health
- Purpose and meaning

Today's workplaces are largely becoming supportive platforms where individuals can enhance their wellbeing and utilize their talents, skills, and ambitions to reach their goals. And the benefits extend to not only the employees but also the overall organization, influencing its future profitability. But we still have plenty of work to do.

Summary

Companies seek high-performing employees who can efficiently complete their tasks and achieve their assigned goals. It's clear that a healthy and well-engaged workforce performs at an impressively higher level (Wellbeing at Work 27), so companies should prioritize investments in wellbeing. As you reflect on your organization, consider which steps you're currently taking to boost employee well-being. Do you have a dedicated strategy for addressing mental health and wellbeing? One fundamental goal of any workplace should be to cultivate an environment where every individual can flourish—Enhancing a person's wellbeing is key to unlocking their best performance. A thriving organization benefits from employees who are performing at their best, as it directly impacts their bottom line.

Chapter Takeaways

- Positive psychology, which is rooted in evidence-based research, aims to optimize work performance and create a more positive workplace culture.

- Leveraging strengths is crucial for professional development and workplace motivation, and assessments like the VIA Character Strengths can help employees identify their core values and energizers.

- Promoting employee well-being, including physical health, emotional satisfaction, financial stability, mental health, and a sense of purpose, is essential for organizational success and performance.

- Companies should prioritize investments in employee wellbeing to create an environment where individuals can flourish and perform at their best.

Checkpoint

1. Reflect on your organization's leadership approach. How can you ensure it goes beyond Taylorism and considers the wellbeing and fulfillment of your employees?

2. Consider your well-being at work, including your physical health, emotional satisfaction, financial stability, mental health, and sense of purpose and meaning. How can you

prioritize these aspects? How might they contribute to your overall performance and success?

3. As a leader/manager, what steps can you take to promote greater wellbeing within your team? How might this positively impact team performance and the organization as a whole?

CHAPTER 5

Positive Experiences

Positive Experiences

"If you look good, you feel good. If you feel good, you play good. If you play good, they pay good."
—Deion Sanders, NFL Hall of Famer

My friend Nicole is a talented business analyst at a small community bank. She's great at her job, yet every Sunday evening, she's gripped by anxiety as she braces herself for Monday—a phenomenon some call the "Sunday Scaries." Over the past year, her relationships with her manager and coworkers have suffered. Although she's frequently praised for her efforts at work, the negative incidents far outweigh the positive ones. Recently, her manager scolded her for submitting a report a day late. On another occasion, her colleagues laughed at her idea for a project. These experiences are not only escalating her anxiety attacks, but they're also affecting her job performance. She thought about taking this to HR, but she's worries it might worsen her situation.

The sobering reality is that Nicole's story is far from unique. In a recent workplace culture article by EBN, the latest statistics reveal that 60% of employees have encountered negative experiences in the work environment within the last month. These situations can worsen employees' mental health issues and hamper productivity. Workplace stress and conditions like anxiety or depression often stem from sustained negative experiences and inadequate management strategies. Prolonged exposure to such negativity often leads to absenteeism, and in the long run, to two-week notices. This was true for Nicole. Initially, she began calling in sick more often. Then, she looked for a new job. Organizations must work harder to understand and create positive work environments if they want to retain their best and brightest employees.

A positive workplace isn't just about accolades and promotions. It's also about fostering an environment where employees can cultivate joy, happiness, love, support, empathy, kindness, optimism, and fairness. It's about how people feel when they're at work. We humans are wired to focus on negative aspects, and let's face it: Work isn't going to be all sunshine and rainbows—but it shouldn't be all doom and gloom either.

We need more leaders who understand the importance of cultivating positive experiences at work. Organizations should commit to this not only because it boosts productivity and benefits the bottom line, but because it's the ethical choice to make. The workplace should be a setting where people feel respected and valued.

The Broaden-and-Build Theory of Positive Emotions

Employees want to have fulfilling experiences at work. Positive psychology professor Barbara Frederickson introduced a key concept for understanding this innate desire, which is known as the broaden-and-build theory. She suggested that positive emotions not only lead to more positive emotions, but they also equip us with social, physical, intellectual, and psychological resources. So, how is this theory relevant to organizations? Employees who feel good at work also become more:

- Creative
- Innovative
- Optimistic
- Resilient
- Supportive

These qualities are the hallmarks of high-performing employees, effective teams and healthy company cultures. On the other hand, negative emotions build walls around individuals. An employee who shows up to work in a foul mood or experiences a lot of negativity once they get there is unlikely to perform well.

One particular study underscores the impact of positive emotions. Participants were split into two groups. One group watched uplifting, joyful movies that fostered positive emotions, while the other saw films that stirred anger, darkness, and negativity. The outcome was enlightening: Those who viewed the positive movies were significantly better at solving problems and felt more optimistic about the future. In a nutshell, promoting positive emotions at work isn't just a nicety; it's a necessity if you want your organization to grow and perform its best.

The Positivity Tipping Point

What forms the foundation of a positive experience at work? A culture that's rooted in positive emotions! Evidence from the realm of positive psychology indicates that employees are more productive, effective and collaborative when their ratio of positive-to-negative work experiences is 3-to-1. Research on 60 teams by Lossada in 1999 found a clear difference in performance based on this ratio: Low-performing teams had a 1:1 positive-to-negative ratio, average teams had a 2:1 ratio, and high-performing teams hit the tipping point with a 3:1 ratio. These findings revealed a stark contrast between teams that were merely getting by and those that were truly thriving.

To achieve this 3:1 positivity ratio, it's crucial to foster positive interactions among leaders, managers, and colleagues. Take, for instance, a manager at a local nonprofit who kicks off his weekly team meetings by encouraging members to share a personal and a professional highlight. This simple practice infuses positivity into the team's atmosphere and demonstrates his personal interest in them. Although they tackle difficult issues during the meetings, starting on a positive note encourages kindness, gratitude, fairness, celebration, hope, and optimism. And when employees feel good, they tend to be more creative, logical, and focused on their tasks.

The Impact of Virtuous Acts

Creating a positive workplace experience isn't just about internal dynamics. Reaching out to the community can also play a vital role! Providing volunteer opportunities for employees to donate their time or resources to meaningful causes can foster a sense of fulfillment. There's something rewarding about giving to others, and when this takes place within a workplace context, it can help strengthen bonds and elevate the overall experience. For example, one organization I know dedicates an entire month to supporting a local nonprofit, encouraging employees to participate in community cleanup efforts and contribute financially. These activities spark joy and boost satisfaction within employees, reinforcing the sense that they're making a meaningful contribution to their community.

But virtuous acts aren't confined to external endeavors. Fostering an environment of generosity and kindness within the organization can significantly enhance the workplace experience, too. Such an environment not only boosts the morale of employees but also translates to better interactions with customers. Research has linked these acts with improved organizational performance and elevated outcomes. Organizations that habitually engage in acts of virtue set the stage for thriving, positive work environments. At their core, virtuous acts can help individuals and organizations be their best selves, meaningfully impacting both the employees and the broader community.

The Power of Forgiveness

One surefire way to enhance an employee's experience is through the act of forgiveness. There will inevitably be moments when employees royally screw up a project, underperform, or gossip about their supervisor or coworker. Instances like these can breed resentment and undermine trust within teams and organizations. However, fostering a culture of forgiveness can counteract these effects and create a positive work experience. People need to know that if they stumble, they won't face humiliation or miss out on opportunities to make things right. A strengths-based approach involving forgiveness is a potent predictor of job satisfaction and contributes significantly to a positive culture.

Summary

Employees who have more positive experiences at work tend to perform better and engage more fully in their roles. Organizations should strive to cultivate a positive mood among their staff, as it can boost creativity and innovation. Moreover, building a positive work culture is paramount for employees to truly thrive. In addition to positive experiences, the quality of workplace relationships is also crucial for the overall wellbeing of individuals. Such positive relationships often drive employees' long-term commitment to an organization!

Chapter Takeaways

- A positive workplace fosters joy, happiness, support, empathy, kindness, optimism, and fairness, allowing employees to feel valued and respected.

- Research suggests that a 3-1 ratio of positive-to-negative work experiences is optimal for creating high-performing teams.

- Engaging in virtuous acts, both internally and in the community, strengthens bonds and contributes to a more meaningful workplace experience.

- Forgiveness is important for building a positive work culture and fostering trust between team members.

- Organizations need to create positive work environments to retain talented employees and improve productivity.

Checkpoint

1. Can you think of a time when a positive interaction significantly improved your workplace experience? How could such acts become a more regular part of your organization's culture?

2. Now, bring to mind a negative interaction from the past. What went south? How was it resolved?

3. How do you encourage positive relationships between members of your team? In what ways have these relationships directly affected your employees' commitment to your organization?

4. What's your organizational culture like? What initiatives or changes could you introduce to improve it? Which ones could you retire?

5. How do you think your employees would describe their overall experience at work? What steps can you take to ensure they have more positive than negative experiences?

CHAPTER 6

Social Connection

Social Connection

"The quality of our relationships determine the quality our lives."
—Esther Perel, Belgium-American Psychotherapists

An organization's culture can only be as healthy as its interactions between coworkers. Even in our increasingly virtual work environment, positive workplace relationships remain essential for flourishing. This doesn't imply everything must always go smoothly either. On the contrary, it's through challenging conversations, conflicts, and misunderstandings that we uncover the true strength of our relationships. Improving relationships can only occur when the individuals involved are willing to overcome conflicts, extend forgiveness, and empathize with each other. This dynamic affects not only employees' wellbeing but also greatly influences the company's ability to achieve its goals and desired outcomes.

High-Quality Connections

Certain work relationships energize you, and interacting with these colleagues makes you feel motivated and alive. Positive psychologists refer to these life-giving relationships as high-quality connections, which are critical to the success of any organization and individual's wellbeing. After all, the way people interact is the secret sauce for accomplishing tasks within any organization. In her book *Positive Psychology at Work*, Sarah

Lewis outlines three characteristics of high-quality connections based on her research:

1. Their ability to handle emotions
2. Their ability to bounce back from setbacks
3. Their degree of connectivity

When you share a strong and positive emotional connection with someone, it's easier to express yourself. These trusted individuals, also known as high-quality connectors, will not only celebrate your achievements in the workplace, such as a promotion, but they'll also support you during times of disappointment, like when a deal you've been working on for months falls through.

Every relationship experiences conflict, whether minor or significant, but how you address this conflict determines whether the relationship is a high-quality connection. Quick recovery from hurt feelings, misunderstandings, or offenses is a sign of a positive relationship. Strong connectivity fosters forgiveness, allowing people to express disappointment, heal, and ultimately form a stronger bond.

Connectivity between coworkers can also facilitate the exchange of information, new ideas, and influence. These connections promote a sense of freedom and support in the workplace, increase engagement, and facilitate more connection between managers and team members. High-quality connections also have a powerful psychological effect, enabling people to overcome stress more easily and rely on their network for support. The bottom line? High-quality connections ultimately impact *your organization's* bottom line.

A Best Friend at Work

Consider Sarah, who's an accountant for a mid-sized public relations firm, and her friend Kelly, who works on the marketing side. Over the years, they've cultivated a strong friendship. They spend much of their free time together, carpool, take weekend trips, and even pet-sit for each other when necessary. Recently, Sarah received offers from larger accounting firms. However, she's been delaying her decision because she values her current workplace's culture and doesn't want to leave Kelly behind. She understands that it's the type of relationship that's rare to find.

An article by Gallup entitled "The Increasing Importance of a Best Friend at Work" demonstrates that having a best friend at work has become more crucial since the pandemic onset, despite the dramatic increase in remote and hybrid work. This suggests that people value authentic, supportive relationships both at work and in life. Notably, Gallup reports that Millennials, who are predicted to constitute 43% of the workforce by 2025, are twice as likely to be engaged at work if they have a friend (63%), compared to those who do not (29%).

It's evident that having a best friend at work significantly contributes to your wellbeing. Positive, healthy relationships leave a lasting impact on work performance. A best friend at work not only enhances the overall atmosphere of the organizational culture but also encourages commitment, often causing individuals to prioritize relationships over other opportunities, like higher pay.

Belonging

When people feel valued, accepted, and connected to their work community, they experience a sense of belonging – and one of the most detrimental barriers to nurturing positive and healthy relationships is isolating an employee. If an individual feels ostracized, they often feel constant anxiety, which means their work performance will inevitably suffer. Leaders should strive to find ways to include all employees within their work culture, celebrating the unique attributes each person brings to the organization. With the current trend of remote work, it becomes even more crucial to intentionally foster inclusion. In fact, one company I've worked with in the past invites each new employee to spend 10-15 minutes introducing themselves by discussing their favorite hobby. The aim is to encourage coworkers to build relationships based on shared interests.

Another essential element in fostering a sense of belonging among employees is embracing workforce diversity. In his book *Belonging: The Science of Creating Connection and Bridging Divides*, Geoffrey L. Cohen writes, "Of all the threats to belonging, longstanding problems of discrimination are among the most potent and pressing." Blatant discrimination in hiring practices, awarding promotions, and filling leadership positions can inhibit relationships and cultivate a negative culture. Your organization must actively practice anti-discrimination in both word and deed to truly embrace and celebrate diversity.

The Fish Philosophy

The Fish Philosophy, which originates from the Pike Place Fish Market in Seattle, provides an excellent framework for developing positive work relationships and high-quality connections. Its four pillars encapsulate how to build these connections:

1. **Be there.** Be present and fully engaged with others. Pay careful attention, avoid distractions, and respond positively to the person you're interacting with.
2. **Make their day.** Aim to make everyday interactions with colleagues pleasant. A smile, a kind word, or even just a friendly hello can make a significant difference. Be intentional and positive in your interactions.

3. **Play.** Laughter is a powerful tool for building relationships. Not all tasks need to be serious. Demonstrating a playful side and not always taking yourself too seriously can improve the workplace atmosphere. Shared laughter releases oxytocin in the body, fostering feelings of relaxation and bonding. Organizations should promote workplace fun, events, and celebrations, while being mindful of those who may feel threatened or uncomfortable due to social anxiety.

4. **Choose your attitude.** Adopting a positive outlook can generate energy and optimism about what is possible. Focus on recognizing each other's strengths in the workplace and capitalizing on what is already working well. More positive outcomes result from leveraging these strengths and maintaining a positive attitude.

Summary

In conclusion, positive workplace relationships are pivotal to cultivating a healthy organizational culture. It's important to emphasize meaningful interactions between colleagues, even in the realm of remote work, are crucial for both personal and organizational success. In this chapter we also highlight concept of "high-quality connections" as relationships that invigorate and motivate individuals. It underscores the benefits of high-quality connection in exchanging information, facilitating innovation, and contributing to improved employee well-being and engagement.

The Fish philosophy is introduced as framework for building positive work relationships, principles of being present, making others' day better, infusing playfulness, and maintaining a positive attitude.

Chapter Takeaways

- Positive workplace relationships are crucial for organizational culture and success, even in virtual work environments.

- High-quality connections characterized by emotional handling, resilience, and connectivity are essential for individual and organizational flourishing.

- Having a best friend at work significantly contributes to employee wellbeing and engagement.

- Fostering a sense of belonging and embracing diversity is crucial for nurturing positive and healthy relationships.

- The Fish Philosophy emphasizes presence and, making others people's day, through playfulness, and positive attitudes as key elements for building positive work relationships.

Checkpoint

1. How would you assess the quality of connections among your team members? What actions have you taken to foster high-quality connections? What actions could you take?

2. How does your organization embrace diversity?

3. How does your organization address discrimination? Are there explicit anti-discrimination practices in place?

4. Reflecting on the Fish Philosophy, which of the four pillars do you believe your organization embodies well? Which pillars could use improvement?

CHAPTER 7

Meaningful Work

Meaningful Work

"The purpose in life is not to be happy. It is to be useful, to be honorable, to be compassionate, to have it make some difference that you have lived and lived well."
—*Ralph Waldo Emerson, American Philosopher*

A while back, a close friend asked me, "What does finding meaning at work even mean?" I considered his question carefully and then told him that meaningful work typically revolves around our core values, calling, and community. If our sole purpose for work is to gain money or status, life will become thoroughly unsatisfying. Instead, our work should positively contribute to our well-being in some way.

Although an increasing number of companies recognize the importance of meaningful work, many leaders still have no clue how to implement it in their workplaces. Modern workers are becoming more aware of the importance of infusing their work with meaning, rather than just working for a paycheck, so the future of the workforce hinges on workers finding significance and feeling like their work makes a substantial contribution to their organization and community.

Core Values

When considering what meaningful work might look like for you, look no further than your core values, which are a significant indicator of what's important to you. You can't separate your values from who you are at work; after all, they shape your worldview! That's why it's vital to identify and understand them. Getting clear on your core values will inform your decision-making process, including whether you'll accept a particular job, if you'll join a specific organization, and what will bring you purpose in your work.

It's not only important to know your core values but also how and where these values align with those of your organization. Your ability to live out these values in your workplace will be a key component of finding more meaning at work. Some examples of core values are:

- Diversity and inclusion
- Innovation
- Growth
- Trust
- Fairness
- Competitiveness
- Community

Once you know your values, you can find ways to express them at work. So, how do you identify your core values? Write them down! If you're not sure where to start, use the list that's available at scottjefferey.com/core-values-list. Choose the 5-7 values that resonate most with you.

My Core Values

1. _______________________________

2. _______________________________

3. _______________________________

4. _______________________________

5. _______________________________

6. _______________________________

7. _______________________________

Another effective core value exercise is to consider someone you genuinely admire or wish to emulate. Spend some time writing down the characteristics you appreciate most about this person and perceive as their finest qualities. Then, identify the values you aspire to embody! It doesn't matter which exercise you choose; the point is to reflect on the behaviors, attitudes, or qualities you wish to display in your workplace.

Calling vs. Career

A calling is the pursuit of a higher purpose. Embracing your passions and interests or leveraging your strengths at work will result in a deeper sense of meaning than simply clocking in and out. When employees discover their calling, they understand their roles within their workplace and often become the top performers on their teams. You can further explore the difference between a calling and a career in the chart below.

Career	Calling
Employees prioritize pay and advancement	Employees see their work as a positive end in and of itself
Employees are only happy if they are "winning"	Employees derive satisfaction from their work and relationships with coworkers
Employees get overly concerned when they are not advancing	Employees are happy, fulfilled *and* successful
Employees are always chasing something new	Employees genuinely feel good about the work they're doing

As you can see, a calling provides a clearer path to fulfillment and meaning than a mere career. Be sure to give yourself time to discover your calling. This process often involves navigating through various jobs, determining what kind of work energizes you, and identifying what tasks drain you. Eventually, you'll recognize which skills and abilities complement your true calling and how best to live out that calling in your workplace.

Community

After reflecting on your core values and calling, ask yourself, "Am I engaged in work that positively impacts my community?" Take my friend Josh, who was diagnosed with irritable bowel syndrome in his youth. He faced significant challenges, including extreme stomach pain, swelling, and bloating after eating certain foods and his condition greatly impacted his social life, since food is often a central part of socializing for young people. In college, Josh found purpose in a nutrition class, deciding to become a nutritionist so he could help others navigate similar experiences.

Yet after college, Josh struggled to find a job as a nutritionist and worked various odd jobs for several years. Just as he was about to give up on his dream, he found a nonprofit that educated high school students about nutrition and offered wellness coaching. This role gave Josh a renewed sense of purpose in his life because he felt he was making a difference in his community while doing the work he loved.

At an organizational level, leaders need to provide avenues for employees to engage in prosocial practices and help others within their community. Ultimately, we need to feel like our work is making a difference. When we can see the results of our work and the people we've helped, we naturally find more meaning in our efforts. And there's no better feeling than knowing you've improved another person's life through your work!

The Benefits of Meaningful Work

Meaningful work is more than warm fuzzies, though. Over time, it can seriously improve an organization by:

- Fostering high intrinsic motivation
- Enhancing job satisfaction
- Reducing employee absenteeism and turnover
- Cultivating more committed workers
- Boosting employee engagement and performance

Although finding more meaning at work can be a complex pursuit, the elements we've discussed provide a solid framework. When our employees aspire to find more meaning in their work, it's our responsibility to do our utmost to equip them with the tools necessary for this discovery.

Summary

There is a growing awareness among workers about the importance of seeking meaning at work rather than simply pursing monetary gain. The significance of aligning personal values with organizational values create a sense of purpose and fulfillment in the workplace. In addition, this chapter explores the distinction between a career and a calling, highlighting how embracing a calling leads to deeper fulfillment and contribution.

Chapter Takeaways

- Meaningful work revolves around core values, callings, and community involvement, which contributes to individual wellbeing and satisfaction.

- Identifying and understanding their core values is a crucial component of an employee's decision-making process and alignment with organizational values.

- Embracing a calling, pursuing a higher purpose, and leveraging passions can result in finding deeper meaning and fulfillment at work.

- Engaging in work that positively impacts the community fosters a sense of purpose and allows individuals to see the results of their efforts.

- Meaningful work brings numerous benefits, including increased job satisfaction, commitment, engagement, and performance, while reducing absenteeism and turnover.

Checkpoint

1. How do your core values align with those of your organization, and how does this alignment contribute to your sense of meaning at work? How can you help employees identify and align their core values with those of the organization?

2. Do you have processes in place to promote and celebrate the "calling" aspect of work rather than just viewing it as a career or a means to an end? In what ways does your organization foster a sense of purpose and calling among employees?

3. How does your organization encourage prosocial behavior and contribute positively to the community?

4. What further steps can you take to make work more meaningful for your employees, and how will you go about implementing these changes?

CHAPTER 8

Flourishing

Flourishing

"Change is essential to growth. Embrace the unpredictability, accept your own painful process, and know opinion can never take away your personal truth. Allow yourself to flourish into a matured, improved version of yourself, but know that it takes time."

—Kristen Michelle Elizabeth, Author of *This Will Set Me Free*

As far as employee performance and development goes, engagement is often considered to be the holy grail—and while it matters, it shouldn't be your end goal. For your organization and employees to perform their best, it's vital to find ways to help them move beyond being merely engaged at work to *flourishing* at work.

So what does flourishing look like? In his book *Positive Organizations*, Robert E. Quinn defines *flourishing* as: *"growing, thriving, exceeding expectations, and moving toward excellence."* For your organization to achieve its full potential, you must first empower your employees to unlock *their* full potential. Because when employees begin to flourish, every other aspect of your organization follows suit—from culture and innovation to business outcomes and client relationships. So, how can we help more employees flourish at work?

Go With the Flow

My good friend Carlos, who's a software engineer, once told me that he often gets so engrossed in his programming work, he loses track of time and forgets to take breaks or even to go to lunch. He said that whenever this happens, he feels most alive, focused, confident, and competent. This experience isn't unique to coders either. Athletes may call it "a runner's high" or "sailing with the wind." To writers or musicians, it's "becoming one with the music." In his book *Flow,* Mihaly Csikszentmihalyi refers to this phenomenon as a *flow experience,* or "the state in which people are so involved in an activity that nothing else seems to matter; the experience itself is so enjoyable that people will do it even at great cost, for the sheer sake of doing it." He outlines three keys to unlocking it:

1. A clearly defined set of goals
2. A balance between perceived challenges and perceived skills, where both exceed the person's average levels so that the challenges stretch the skills (but not by too much)
3. Clear and immediate feedback

A common pitfall in many workplaces is that employees become bored, apathetic, or too comfortable in their roles. To truly flourish, employees need to be challenged and feel that they are growing in their positions. One way managers and leaders can combat this stagnation is to facilitate situations where workers can navigate new challenges that align with their skillset. This can result in more flow experiences. They don't merely feel good for staff either. Organizations also reap tremendous rewards from staff's flow experiences, including better performance, increased productivity, massive growth in their bottom line, a healthier culture, and a higher employee retention rate—just to name a few!

Better Self-Regulation Skills = Better Engagement

When employees can self-regulate, they can monitor and manage their own thoughts, emotions, and behaviors more effectively, which in turn, helps them remain engaged and disciplined. Self-regulation is also an integral element of flourishing as well. Employees who can manage their impulses and distractions are also less likely to get overwhelmed when solving problems and completing tasks.

One of the biggest hindrances to employee engagement is procrastination. According to *Psychology Today*, 20% of people describe themselves as "chronic procrastinators." My colleague John used to claim that he did his best work when he waited until the last minute. While this may be true for John and others, it also leads to a ton of stress, and often, mistakes. Self-regulation also encompasses having the motivation, discipline, and willpower to complete tasks without resorting to procrastination. Instead, a properly self-regulated person will have more effective strategies in place.

Employee Motivation

Flourishing at work requires a mutually beneficial relationship between employees and their companies. Of course, every company aims to achieve its business outcomes, but it's essential to consider what's in it for their employees when they do. Demotivated employees can become cynical, pessimistic, distrustful, lacking in empathy, and may do only the bare minimum to retain their jobs. Their behavior is often counterproductive to organizational flourishing. However, when an organization employs strategies that effectively motivate employees, achieving their goals becomes a more natural process. So, how can organizations motivate their staff?

The Self-Determination Theory explores intrinsic motivation and engagement in inherently rewarding activities, proposing that people are motivated to grow and change when these three innate needs are met:

1. **Autonomy:** Employees need to feel like they are in control of their own behavior and goals, and they crave the freedom to complete their work in the way that best suits them. Overly micromanaging and demanding leaders often undermine

employee motivation when they intend to do the exact opposite.

2. **Competence:** When employees have the skills and expertise to contribute effectively to their companies, they experience a greater sense of satisfaction and accomplishment. And if skill deficits do exist, the organization should provide opportunities for reskilling and upskilling.

3. **Connection/Relatedness:** When employees can form friendships and feel like they belong at work, it enhances their motivation.

Self-Determination

When individuals possess a high level of self-determination, they often experience increased job satisfaction and improved wellbeing. For employees, self-determination usually stems from meaningful support and encouragement, positive interactions with their managers, and the belief that they are growing and making use of their skills at work. Over time, this phenomenon can shape the overall culture, as a culture of wellbeing consists of mentally healthy individuals who are flourishing and capable of being their best selves at work.

However, it's important to understand that while people can be extrinsically motivated by money, status, and admiration, those who tend to flourish over the long term are typically intrinsically motivated. These individuals have a genuine passion for the work they do, and their values align with their internal compass, propelling them to achieve their self-set goals in the workplace. If you want more people to flourish in your organization, it's crucial that you first understand what truly motivates them. As we know, everyone's motivation varies in the workplace. If we want both employees and the organization to thrive, it's imperative to understand these motivations and how they contribute to an employee's ability to flourish.

Summary

In the world of employee performance and development, engagement is often considered crucial, but it shouldn't be the goal. To truly enhance your organization's potential, it's essential to move beyond mere engagement and focus on helping employees flourish at work. This means going beyond the norm and facilitating a state of growth, exceeding expectations and striving for excellence.

Chapter Takeaways

- While engagement is important, we must move beyond it to employee flourishing, which is the key to achieving optimal performance and development.

- Flourishing is growing, thriving, exceeding expectations, and moving towards excellence, with the potential to enhance various aspects of organizations.

- To unlock more productivity, embrace the concept of "flow," where employees can become deeply engrossed in their work and focus with confidence and competence.

- For employees to truly flourish, they need challenges that align with their skillsets, enabling them to navigate new experiences and achieve a state of flow.

- Meeting employees' needs for autonomy, competence, and connection fosters intrinsic motivation, which contributes to their ability to flourish.

Checkpoint

1. What does the concept of "flourishing" mean to you on a personal level? How might it apply to your workplace?

2. Can you identify any employees in your organization who are flourishing? What characteristics or behaviors led you to identify them in this way?

3. Can you think of any specific instances where you or your employees have been in a state of "flow"? What steps can you take as a manager or leader to create more opportunities for your employees to experience it?

4. How does your organization approach the challenges of employee motivation? Which of the strategies discussed in this chapter do you think would be most beneficial for your team?

5. Reflecting on the chapter, how can you promote a higher level of self-determination among your employees?

Final Thoughts

"All the evidence that we have indicates that it is reasonable to assume in practically every human being, and certainly in almost every newborn baby, that there is an active will toward health, an impulse towards growth, or towards self-actualization."
—*Abraham Maslow, American Psychologist*

As we conclude this journey, hopefully it's evident that workplace mental health is an essential element of every employee's ability to flourish. Ultimately, this book's approach boils down to remembering that workers are whole human beings first and foremost — and emotionally healthy employees play an invaluable role in reaching your organizational goals. Today's workforce not only wants to be mentally healthy as individuals, but also to work within environments that help them become their best selves. In addition to raising awareness about workplace wellbeing, my goal for this book was to provide evidence-based strategies that will help your workers flourish. Below, you'll find a refresher on each chapter, along with some key takeaways.

Chapter 1

We analyzed the impact of employers overlooking their employees who are languishing, which is a state of emptiness, void, stagnation, and lack of purpose. These employees often go unnoticed and are stuck in the space between depression and flourishing. Leaders and managers must focus on helping these employees move from languishing to flourishing, ultimately improving productivity and preventing the onset of severe mental illnesses.

Chapter 2

We explored the unfortunate reality that many organizations avoid discussions surrounding mental health issues, which means many employees aren't getting the help they need—and their organizations aren't achieving their full potential either. However, most employees today value mental health services and benefits, because they understand that their wellbeing directly impacts their overall productivity and performance. Organizations need to recognize that mental health conversations belong in the workplace because these issues are already present. Creating environments where employees can thrive is crucial for both individuals' and organizations' success.

Chapter 3

This section emphasized the workplace stigma around mental health, showing its negative impact on employees like Chris. Leaders can combat this by educating their staff, promoting better language for understanding, gaining leadership buy-in, and launching organizational campaigns. These steps can help create a more supportive and compassionate environment where mental health is prioritized, leading to better overall employee wellbeing and healthier workplace culture.

Chapter 4

We discussed a few practical applications of Frederick Taylor's scientific management approach in workplace, along with some of its drawbacks, including its failure to consider an employee's need for fulfillment and wellbeing. In addition, we studied the evolution of traditional psychology and the emergence of a new discipline, positive psychology, which seeks to understand each human's level of optimal functioning and to help foster a state of flourishing within them. This field provides evidence-based strategies for improving workplace experiences and optimizing employee performance.

Chapter 5

This section outlined why creating a positive work environment is essential for fostering employee wellbeing and productivity through the broaden-and-build theory of positive emotions, which emphasizes the role of positivity in enhancing creativity, innovation, and resilience in employees. It advises leaders to aim for a 3:1 ratio of positive to negative experiences if they want to cultivate a high-performing team. Additionally, encouraging virtuous acts and forgiveness within a workplace will not only strengthen staff relationships but also result in a more positive and fulfilling work experience that incentivizes employees to thrive, stick around, and achieve their best performance.

Chapter 6

Here, we further delved into why positive work relationships are crucial for both organizational success and employee wellbeing and how embracing diversity and anti-discrimination is a necessary ingredient of creating inclusive environments. The research is clear: High-quality connections, resilience, and connectivity among employees will enhance organizational productivity and creativity. Having a best friend at work can foster greater engagement and commitment, while also promoting a sense of belonging, which shapes a positive work culture. The Fish Philosophy offers a framework for building these relationships through presence, kindness, playfulness, and positive attitudes. Reflecting on these principles can help your organization assess and improve its workplace dynamics and foster a more positive, supportive culture.

Chapter 7

In this chapter, we learned that meaningful work revolves around core values, calling, and community. Identifying and living out your core values, pursuing a calling that aligns with your passions and strengths, and engaging in work that positively impacts the community around you are all essential if you want to find significance within your workplace. Plus, meaningful work increases intrinsic motivation, job satisfaction, and commitment, while also reducing absenteeism and turnover.

Chapter 8

This chapter studied the need to move beyond mere employee engagement and strive to build a flourishing staff. It highlights the importance state of "flow" where employees are fully immersed and focused on their tasks, leading to better outcomes and performance. It also outlined the Self-Determination Theory, which encourages fostering a work culture that promotes wellbeing and success.

Embracing Change and Preparing for the Future

By the year 2025, Millennials and Gen Z will make up 64% of the global workforce, and by the year 2030, they will make up a staggering 75% of the global workforce. Here's the reality: These generations want to work for organizations that prioritize their mental health and wellbeing in the workplace. It's important that your organization is preparing for the future of the workplace and know that mental health will be paramount. These generations bring a unique perspective and will only want to work for leaders and managers who value a mentally healthy, supportive and inclusive environment.

Adapting to the evolving needs and preferences of Millennials and Gen Z is the key to attracting and retaining top talent. This means organizations will need to embrace workplace mental health quickly and meaningfully and also ensure they are building a culture of wellbeing. Organizations that embrace this paradigm shift will stand out amongst Millennials and Gen Z and will become the clear choice for employment.

The bottom line? Embrace this change because it's the future of the workforce. As an organization, find ways to break down the barriers of mental health stigma, provide high-quality mental health resources, create a psychologically safe environment, and foster a culture the prioritizes well-being. By investing in the mental health of your workforce, your employees will flourish and your organization will thrive. This commitment will also help you usher in more transformative workplace experiences and grow your organization beyond what you ever imagined was possible.

Unleashing Your Potential

In summary, everyone deserves to thrive in their workplace, regardless of their role or title. We spend about approximately one-third of our lifetime at work. That's a lot of time away from our families, friends, homes, and the hobbies we enjoy. As human beings, we naturally seek out growth opportunities and ways to become our best selves. Your organization holds the power to help create such an environment, allowing individuals to be their best selves at work—which makes the time they spend there more meaningful and energizing.

Throughout this book, you've discovered areas where you can enhance the wellbeing of your employees. Some concepts can be implemented right away with minimal resources, relying on your good organizational and management skills and with a positive intention to impact those you supervise (and your organization as whole). In the words of Maya Angelou: "I learned that people will forget what you said and people will forget what you did, but people will never forget how you made them feel." Ask yourself: *How am I making people feel at work? I* hope is that eventually, all of your employees will feel a greater sense of support, encouragement, and positivity in your workplace. Together, let's work to unleash the full potential of every individual in your organization!

Recommended Resources

Websites

- Workplace Mental Health: www.workplacementalhealth.org

- Mental Health America: www.mhanational.org

- Substance Abuse and Mental Health Services:
  www.samhsa.com

- World Health Organization: www.who.int

- American Psychological Association: www.apa.org

- Centers for Disease Control and Prevention: www.cdc.gov

- Positive Psychology Center-University of Pennsylvania:
  http://ppc.sas.upenn.edu

- International Positive Psychology Association:
  http://pippanetwork.org

Books

- *The How of Happiness: A Scientific Approach to Getting the Life You Want* by Sonja Lyumbomirsky

- *Flourish: A Visionary New Understanding of Happiness and Wellbeing* by Martin E. Seligman

- *The Positive Organization: Breaking Free From Conventional Cultures, Constraints and Beliefs* by Robert E. Quinn

- *Positive Psychology in Business: 101 Workplace Ideas and Applications* by Sarah Lewis

- *Wellbeing at Work* by Jim Clifton and Jim Harter

- *The Power of Character Strengths: Appreciate and Ignite Your Positive Personality* by Ryan M Niemic and Robert E. McGrawth

- *Positive Leadership: Strategies for Extraordinary Performance* by Kim S. Cameron

- *Purpose and Meaning in the Workplace* by Bryan J Dik

- *Positivity: Groundbreaking Research to Release Your Inner Optimist and Thrive* by Barbara Frederickson

- *Mindset: The New Psychology of Success* by Carol Dweck

Q&A With the Author

I want to address some common questions I get when I speak to groups, teams, and organizations about workplace mental health. Hopefully, this section will provide more info and speak to some fundamental curiosities you may have as a leader or employee. If you have further questions, please don't hesitate to reach out!

How can I help a coworker who's struggling with a mental health issue?

One of the best ways to help a coworker is to be empathetic and supportive throughout their struggles. If you are relatively close to them, ask what you can do to help fulfill a workplace need. For example, your coworker might need a safe place to share their feelings with you. Pro tip: Avoid trying to diagnose them or telling them what worked for someone else who faced similar mental health struggles. Just offer a listening ear and validate their feelings, then be sure to encourage them to seek help from a licensed mental health professional.

What are some examples of workplace mental health education and training?

To make a truly meaningful organizational impact, you must embed mental health education and training within your workplace culture. Here are some things your organization can do to get started:

1. Host a monthly webinar series on mental health topics.
2. Offer quarterly mental health training.
3. Follow up with mental health coaching.
4. Promote mental health awareness campaigns.
5. Bring in external speakers.
6. Invest in workshops.
7. Facilitate e-learning micro lessons on mental health topics.

How should I approach leadership about updating our mental health policies?

Start by having a conversation with your direct manager about your concerns and ideas. Explain how your organization can update current policies, and support your points with solid research. Also, ask your manager how policy changes typically happen within your organization — and if possible, create a committee that focuses on mental health policies, hopefully championed by someone on the leadership team.

What mental health resources are available for employees?

Most organization has an EAP (Employee Assistance Program), which improves employee access to mental health services, especially for an employee in a full-blown mental health crisis.

You should also check with your manager or human resources officer to learn more about your benefits and resources, such as paid subscriptions to mental health apps. If you feel your organization's EAP is lacking, come prepared with evidence-based ideas and strategies, such as recommending that your organization create partnerships with local mental health providers to get additional mental resources for employees.

How can I get my leadership to take workplace mental health seriously?

While I believe it should be common sense to take care of your staff's mental health in the workplace, this isn't always the case for a lot of leaders. One way to get your point across is to bring in plenty of solid research and business case studies proving that having mentally healthy employees positively impacts an organization's bottom line and overall culture. In addition, you may need to find someone who's in a leadership position to champion your cause for it to be taken seriously.

How can I empower my people to get the mental health support they need?

Pressuring someone to seek help may lead to defensiveness or resentment, so be sure to lead with patience and unwavering support. Make sure every staff member has a good understanding of the comprehensive services your organization offers, then encourage employees to utilize the services that best align with their preferences and schedules.

What are some common signs and symptoms an employee is struggling?

- Withdrawing from the team

- Consistently missing virtual or in-person meetings

- Disengaging from work

- Behaving in a way that's out of character

- Changes in mood or performance

What are some barriers to helping staff move from languishing to flourishing?

- **High workload**: When an employee has too many tasks and responsibilities on their plate, their stress often heightens and/or they burn out.

- **Lack of autonomy:** When an employee has limited control over their work and does not have a say in important decisions that affect them, they often disengage.

- **Inadequate support:** Without the proper resources, guidance, and assistance, many employees struggle to reach their full potential and perform their best.

- **Poor leadership:** Ineffective managers, supervisors, and leaders can often cause more harm than good.
- **Limited growth and development opportunities:** To truly flourish, employees need adequate opportunities for advancement, career development, and upskilling.

What are some ways to assess my staff's mental health?

The most efficient way to determine where your organization stands is to conduct an anonymous, staff-wide wellbeing survey. You can also create focus groups and/or interview individual employees. If you're able, it's best to hire an unbiased professional to administer the assessment and design the best interventions for your organization.

What's the #1 mental health benefit for attracting/retaining high-quality hires?

Most workers want flexibility. If possible, offer customizable benefits and mental health days.

Reinforcement Resources

Want in-person support to create a culture of wellbeing? Let's chat! Below, I've outlined the services I offer to organizations.

1. **Consulting**

   Mental health insights, guidance, and practical strategies for leaders and organizations to build a mentally healthy workforce.

2. **Keynote Speaking**

   Inspiring, thought-provoking, and engaging messages from the author on workplace mental health, fostering a positive culture, and employee wellbeing.

3. **Well-being Workshops and Training**

   Tailored workshops and trainings designed to address specific mental health and wellbeing needs in your organization.

4. **Mental Health Coaching**

   Assistance in improving workplace wellbeing through self-discovery and identifying strengths, values, and interests.

5. **Workplace Mental Health Managers Training**

Equipping managers with the knowledge and skills to support the wellbeing of their team.

For further inquiries, please feel free to contact me via email at Michael@dickersoncg.com | LinkedIn: @mikedickerson10/

Endnotes

Achor, S. (2010). The Happiness Advantage: The Seven Principles of Positive Psychology That Fuel Success and Performance at Work. Crown Publishing.

Anchor, Shawn (2013) before happiness: the 5 hidden keys to achieving success, spreading happiness and sustaining positive change. Ransom House, Inc.

Baumeister, Roy and Tierney, Tony (2012) Willpower: Rediscovering the Greatest Human Strength. Penguin Books.

Bower, T. (2014). Bring Work to Life by Bringing Life to Work: A Guide for Leaders and Organizations. San Francisco, CA. Berrett-Koehler Publishers.

Buck, Sabastian The business case for investing in employee wellbeing. Fast Company, 23 May 2023.

Butler, H., & Hasson, F. (2019). Mental Health and Wellbeing in the Workplace: A Practical Guide for Employers and Employees. Routledge.

Butler-Bowdon, Tom (2007) 50 Psychology Classics: Who We Are, How We Think, What We Do: Insight and inspiration from 50 key books. Brealey Publishing.

Cameron, K. S., Dutton, J.E. & Quinn, R.E.(Eds). (2011). Positive organizational scholarships. Berrett-Koehler Publishers.

Cameron, K.S.(2012). Positive Leadership: Strategies for Extraordinary Performance. Berrett-Koehler Publishers.

Cooper, Cary and Ian Hesketh (2019) Wellbeing at Work: How To Design, Implement and Evaluate An Effective Strategy. Kogan Page. 10. Csikszentmihalyi. M. (1990). Flow: The Psychology of Optimal Experience. New York: Harper & Row.

Dean, B., Biswer-Diener, Robert.(2007) Positive Psychology Coaching: Putting the Science of Happiness to Work for Your Clients. Wiley.

Donaldson,S.I (2011). Applied Positive Psychology: Improving Everyday Life, Health, Schools, Work, and Society. Psychology Press.

Donaldson, Stewart. (2021). Positive Organizational Psychology Interventions. Wiley-Blackwell.

Doman, F. (2018). Authentic Strengths. Authentic Strengths Advantage Press.

Geisler, Jill (2012) Work Happy: What Great Bosses Know. Hachette Book Group.

Grenville-Cleave, B. (2012). Positive Psychology: A practical guide. London: Icon Books.

Green. Suzy (2019). The Positivity Prescription: A 6 week Wellbeing Program Based on The Science of Positive Psychology. Positivity Institute.

Hemmings, Jo. How Psychology Works Book: The Facts Visually Explained. DK, 2018.

Hellman, Chan and Gwinn Casey (2019) Hope Rising: How the Science of Hope Can Change Your Life. Morgan James Publishing.

Joseph, S. (2015). Positive Psychology in Practice: Promoting human flourishing in work, health, education, and everyday life. John Wiley & Sons.

Kaufman, Scott Barry (2020) Transcend: The New Science of Self-Actualization. Penguin Random House, LLC.

Keyes, Corey The Mental Health Continuum: From Languishing to Flourishing in Life. Journal Health and Social Behavior, June 2002.

Krekel, Christian, George Ward, Jan-Emmanuel De Neve, and Council Members: J. Harter, A. Blankson, A. Clark, C. Cooper, J. Lim, P. Litchfield, J. Moss, M. I. Norton, A.V. Whillans, and D. Cooperrider, and D. Mendelwicz. "Employee Well-being, Productivity, and Firm Performance: Evidence and Case Studies." Chap. 5 in Global Happiness and Wellbeing Policy Report, by Global Council for Happiness and Wellbeing, 72–94. New York: Sustainable Development Solutions Network, 2019.

Lewis,S. (2011). Positive Psychology at Work: How Positive Leadership and Appreciative Inquiry Create Inspiring Organizations. John Wiley & Sons.

Lewis,S. (2019). Positive Psychology in Business: 101 Workplace Ideas Applications.Wiley.

Linley, S. Harrington, S. Garcia, N. (2013) The Oxford Handbook of Positive Psychology and Work. Oxford University Press.

Lyubomirsky,S. (2008). The how of happiness: A scientific approach to getting the life you want. Penguin.

Niemiec, R. M., & McGrath, R.E. (2019). The Power of Character Strengths: Appreciate and Ignite Your Positive Personality. VIA Institute of Character.

Passmore, J. (Ed). (2017). The Wiley Blackwell Handbook of the Psychology of Positivity and Strengths-Based Approaches at Work. John Wiley & Sons.

Peterson, Christopher. (2012) Pursuing the Good Life: 100 Reflections on Positive Psychology. Oxford University Press.

Pickeren, W.E. The Psychology Book: Big Ideas Simply Explained. DK, 2018.

Quinn, R.E. (2015). The Positive Organization: Breaking Free from Conventional Constraints, and Beliefs. Berrett-Koehler Publishers.

Quinn, R.E.(2014). The Economics of Higher Purpose: Eight Counterintuitive Steps for Creating a Purpose Driven Organization. Berrett-Koehler Publishers.

Santini, Ziggi Ivan Measuring Positive Mental Health and Flourishing in Denmark: Validation of Mental Health Continuum-Short Form and Cross-Cultural Comparison across Three Countries. Health and Quality Outcomes, vol. 18, no 1, September 2020.

Schulz, Marc and Waldinger, Robert (2023) The Good Life: Lessons From The World's Longest Scientific Study of Happiness. Simon & Schuster.

Witters, Dan and Agrawal, Sangeeta The Economic Cost of Poor Employee Mental Health. Gallup Workplace, 3 September 2022. 36. Zenita, B., Bryan J. Steger, M. (2013). Purpose and Meaning In The Workplace.

About the Author

Michael Dickerson is the CEO and Founder of Dickerson Consulting Group, LLC, a consulting firm specializing in human resources, workplace mental health, and wellbeing. Michael holds a certificate in Applied Positive Psychology from the Flourishing Center in New York, which is one of the world's leading institutions in the field of Positive Psychology. In addition to his work as an entrepreneur and a consultant, Michael has served as a mental health practitioner, educator, and keynote speaker for more than 13 years, where he has trained 3,000+ mental health professionals. Today, his primary focus and passion is helping leaders and organizations cultivate a culture of wellbeing that enables all employees to uncover their unique strengths, find meaning, and flourish at work.